UEFA CHAMPIONS LEAGUE

WINNERS LOGO 1956-2020

COLORING BOOK

REAL MADRID

Has Won the Competition Thirteen Times: (1956-1957-1958-1959-1960-1966-1998-2000-2002-2014-2016-2017-2018).

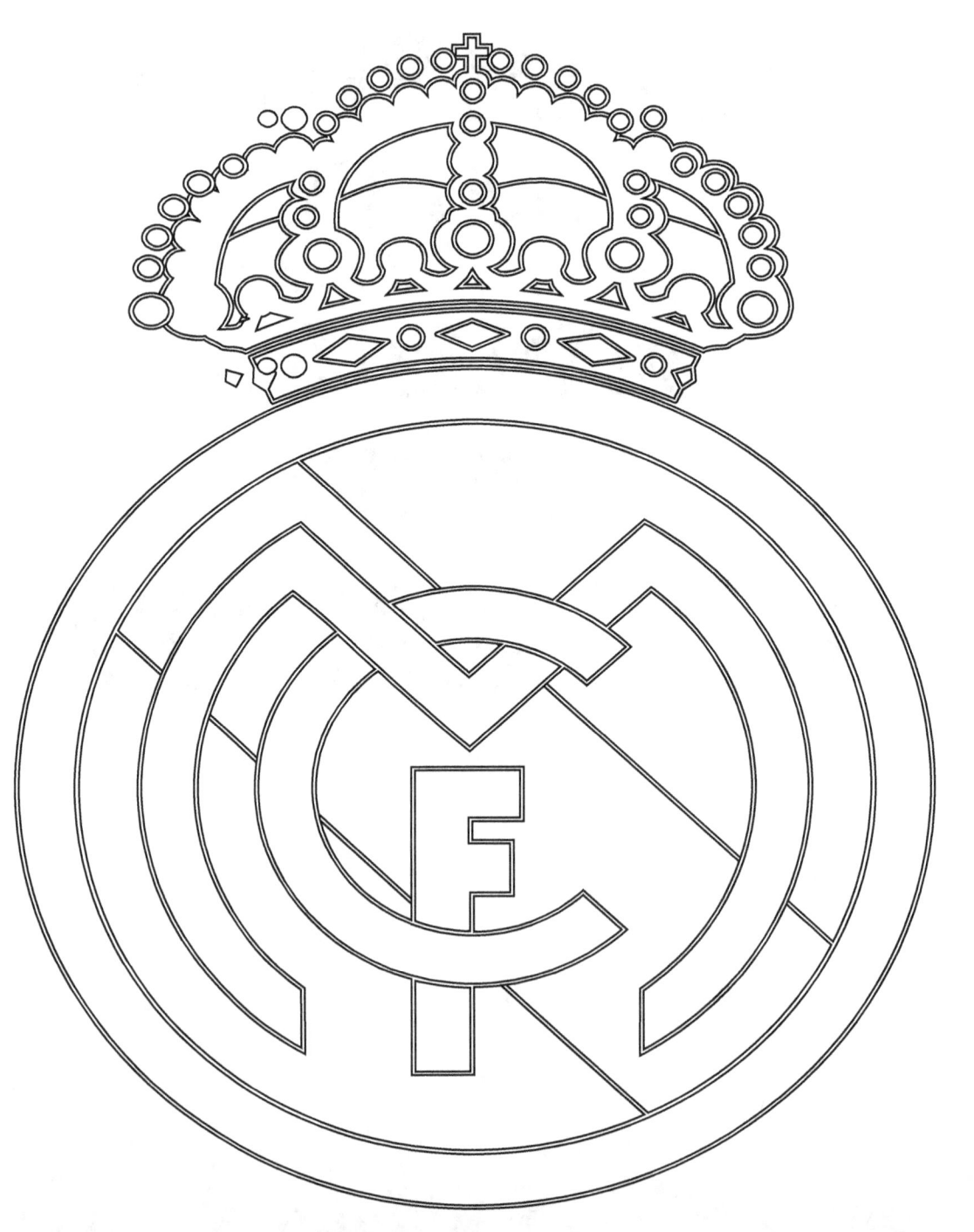

AC MILAN
Has Won the Copmetition Seven Times:
(1963-1969-1989-1990-1994-2003-2007).

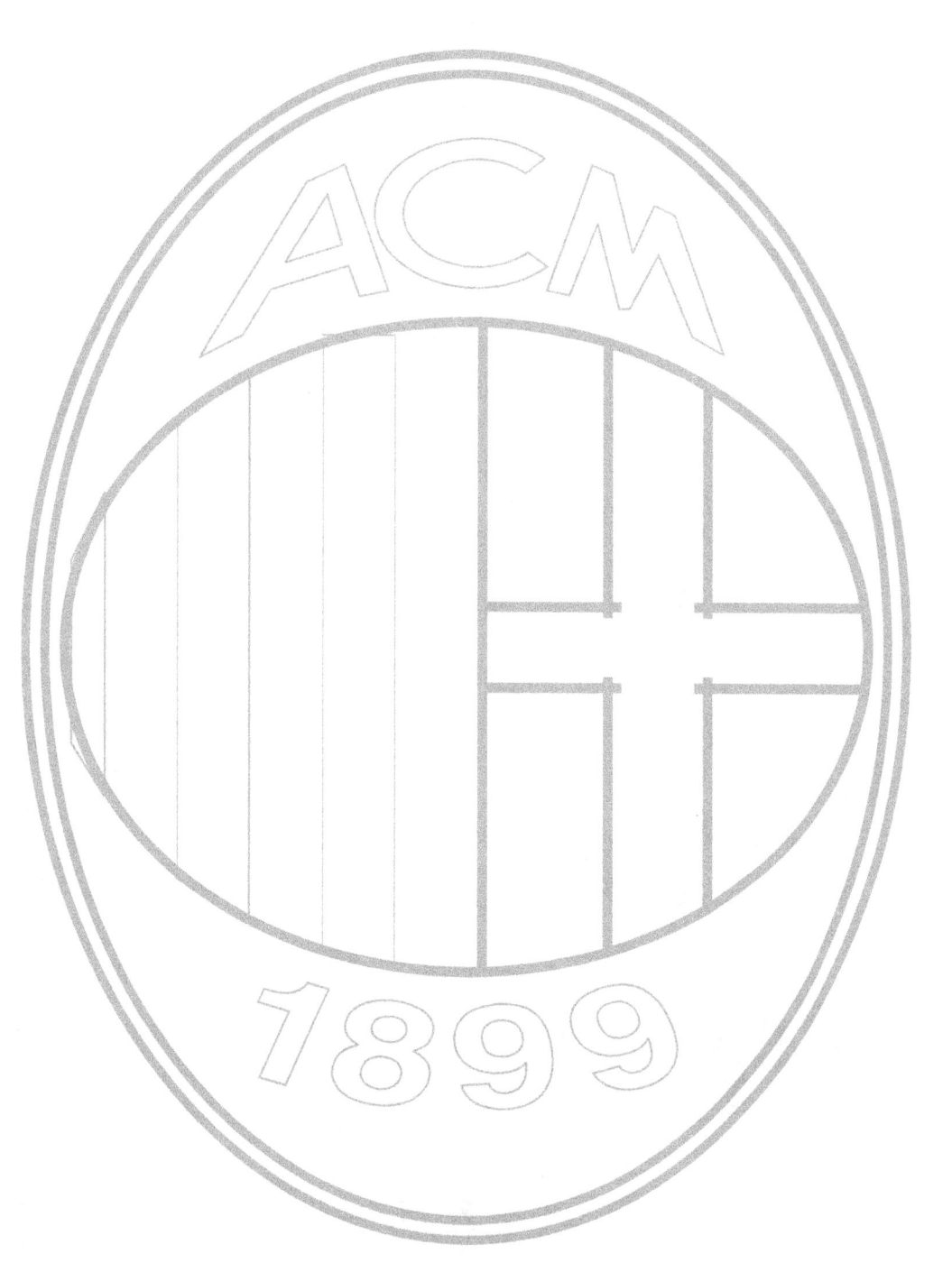

LIVERPOOL FC
Has Won the Competition Six Times: (1977-1978-1981-1984-2005-2019).

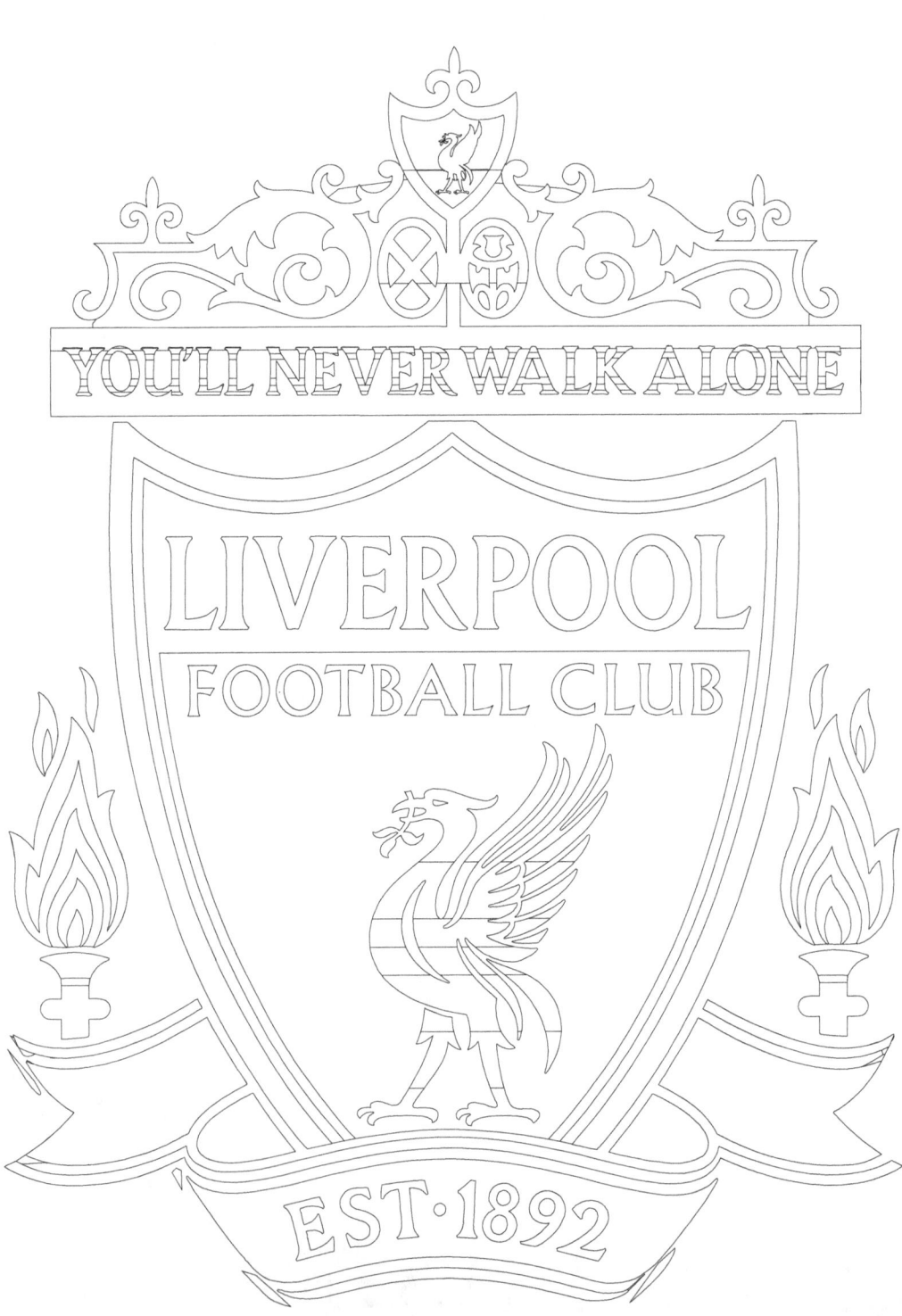

FC BAYERN MUNCHEN
Has Won the Copetition Six Times:
(1974-1975-1976-2001-2013-2020).

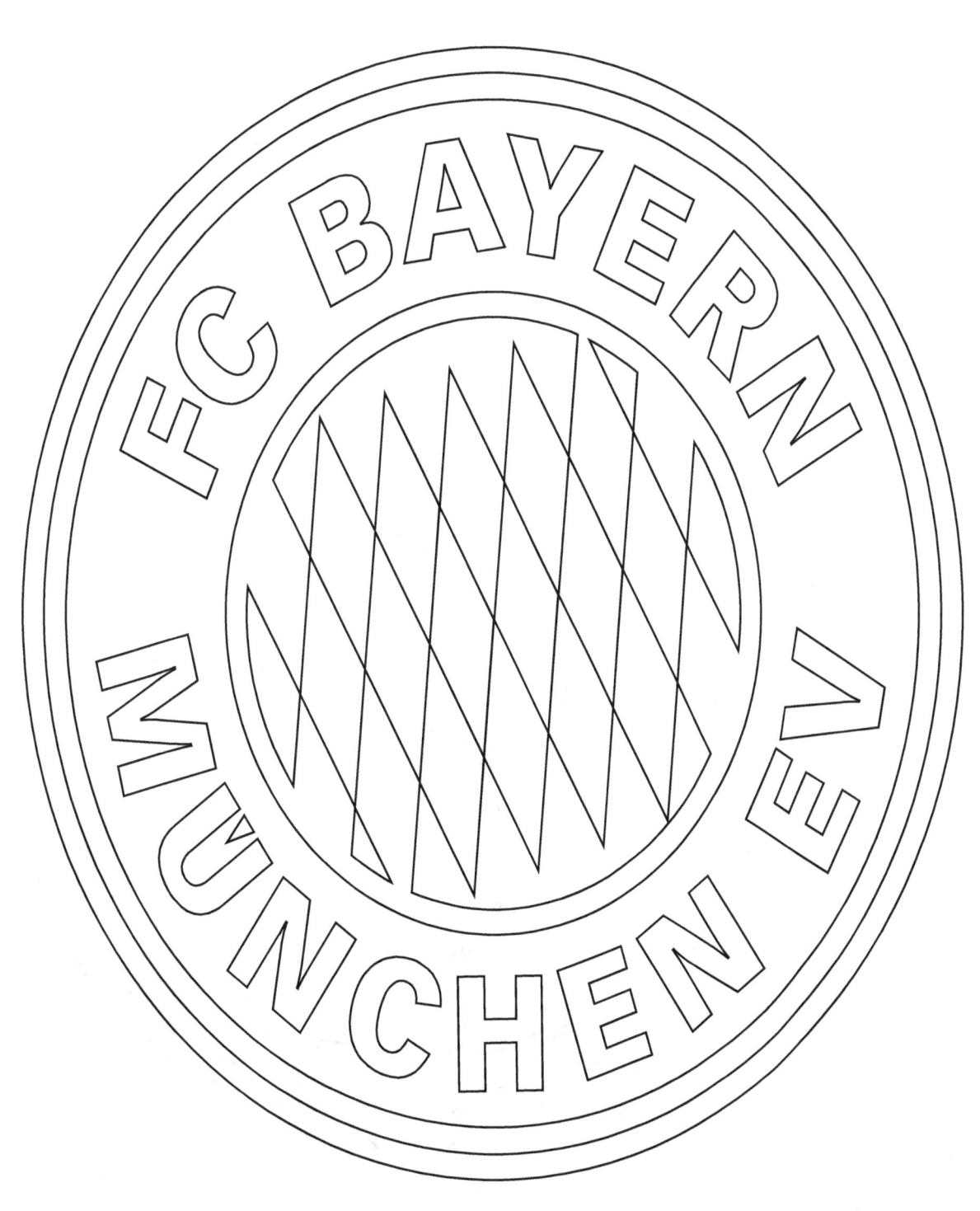

FC BARCELONA
Has Won the Copetition Five Times: (1992-2006-2009-2011-2015).

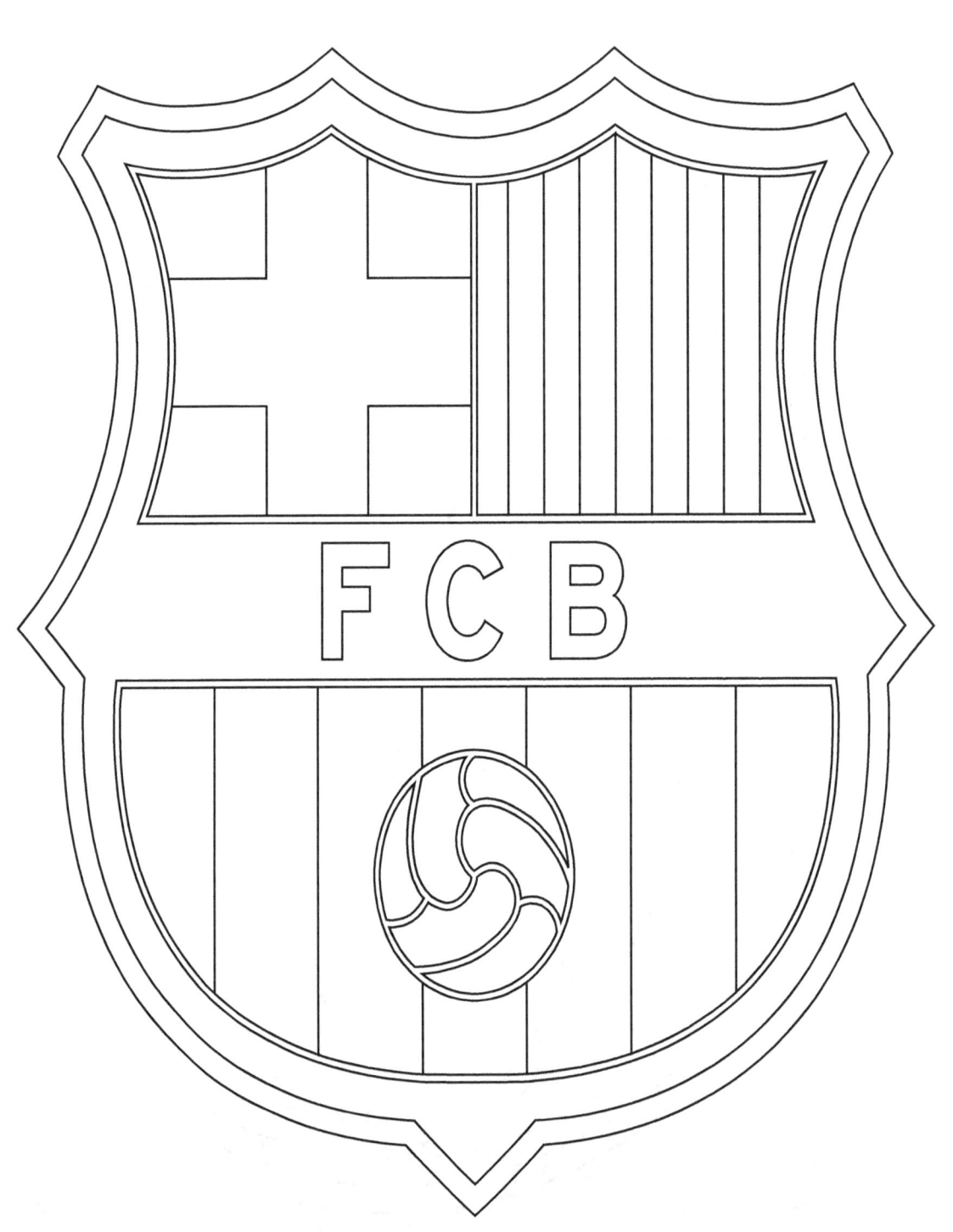

AFC AJAX
Has Won the Copetition Four Times: (1971-1972-1973-1995).

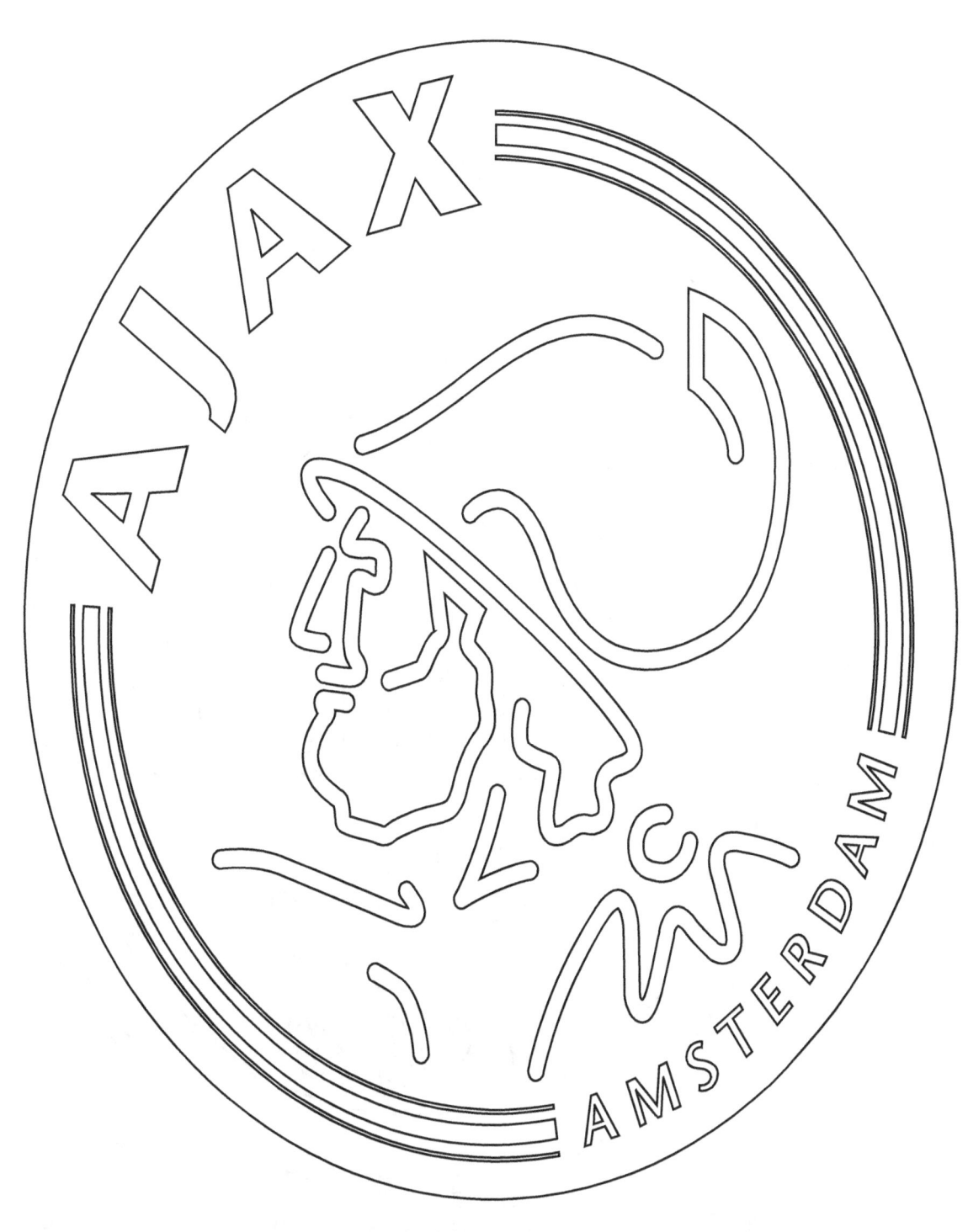

FC INTERNAZIONALE
Has Won the Copetition ThreeTimes: (1964-1965-2010).

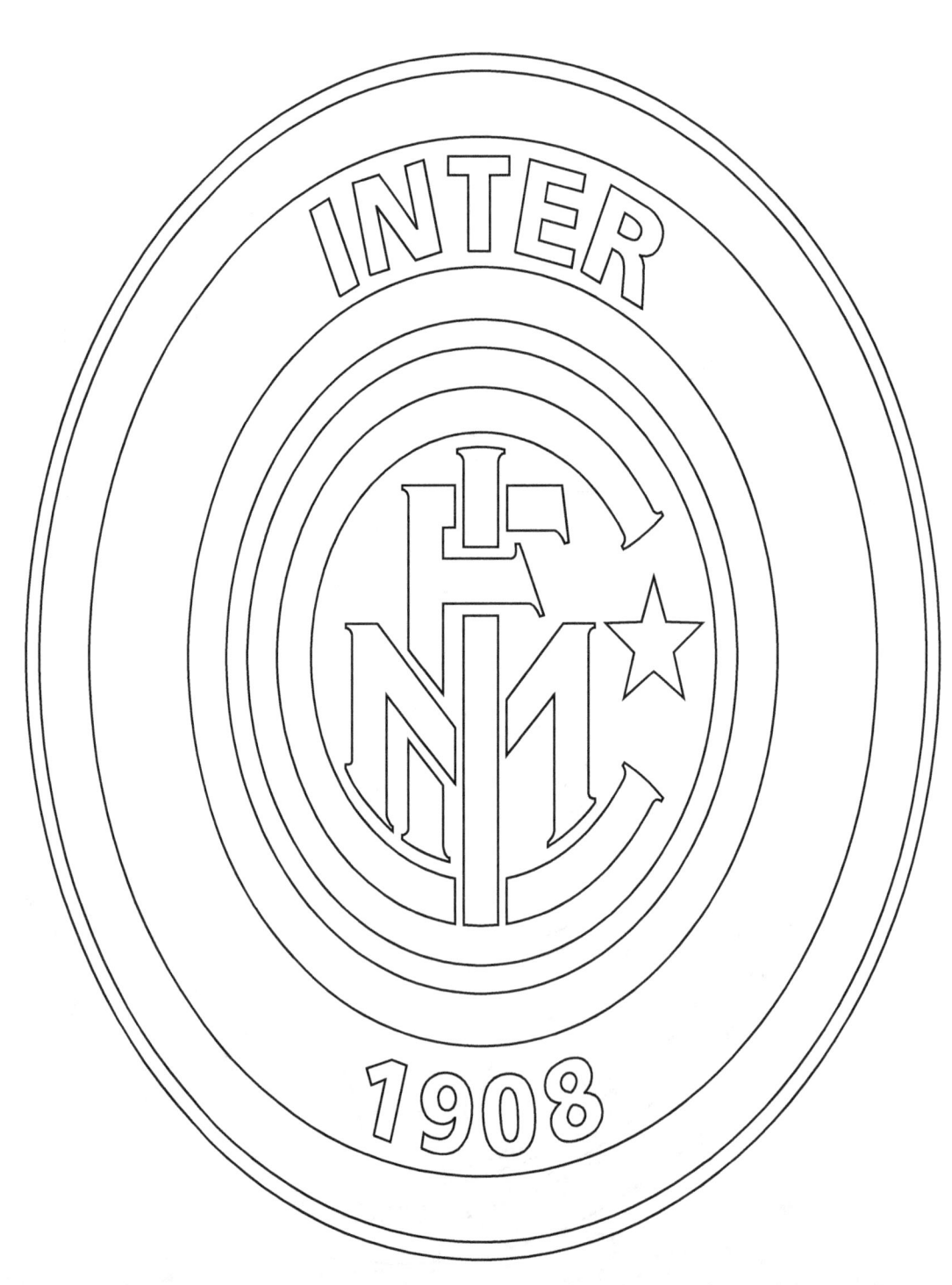

MANCHESTER UNITED
Has Won the Copetition ThreeTimes: (1968-1999-2008).

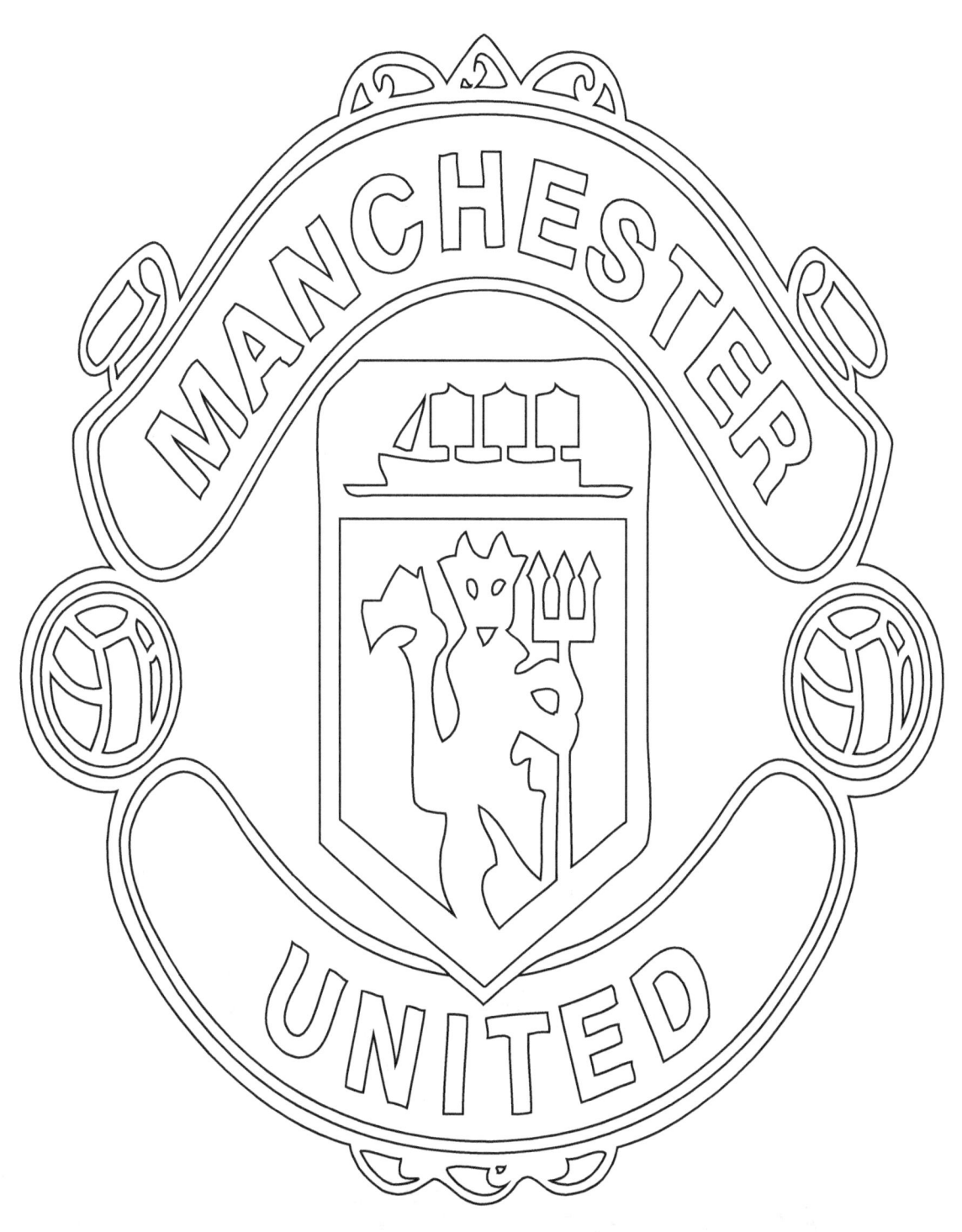

JUVENTUS

Has Won the Copetition TwoTimes: (1985-1996).

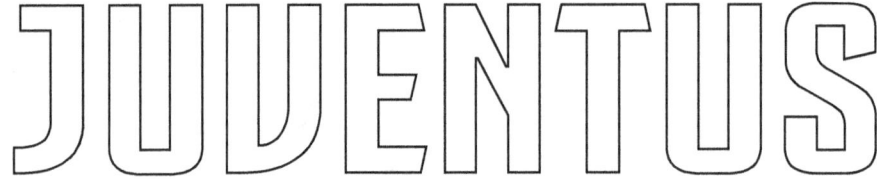

SPORT LISBOA e BENFICA
Has Won the Copetition TwoTimes: (1961-1962).

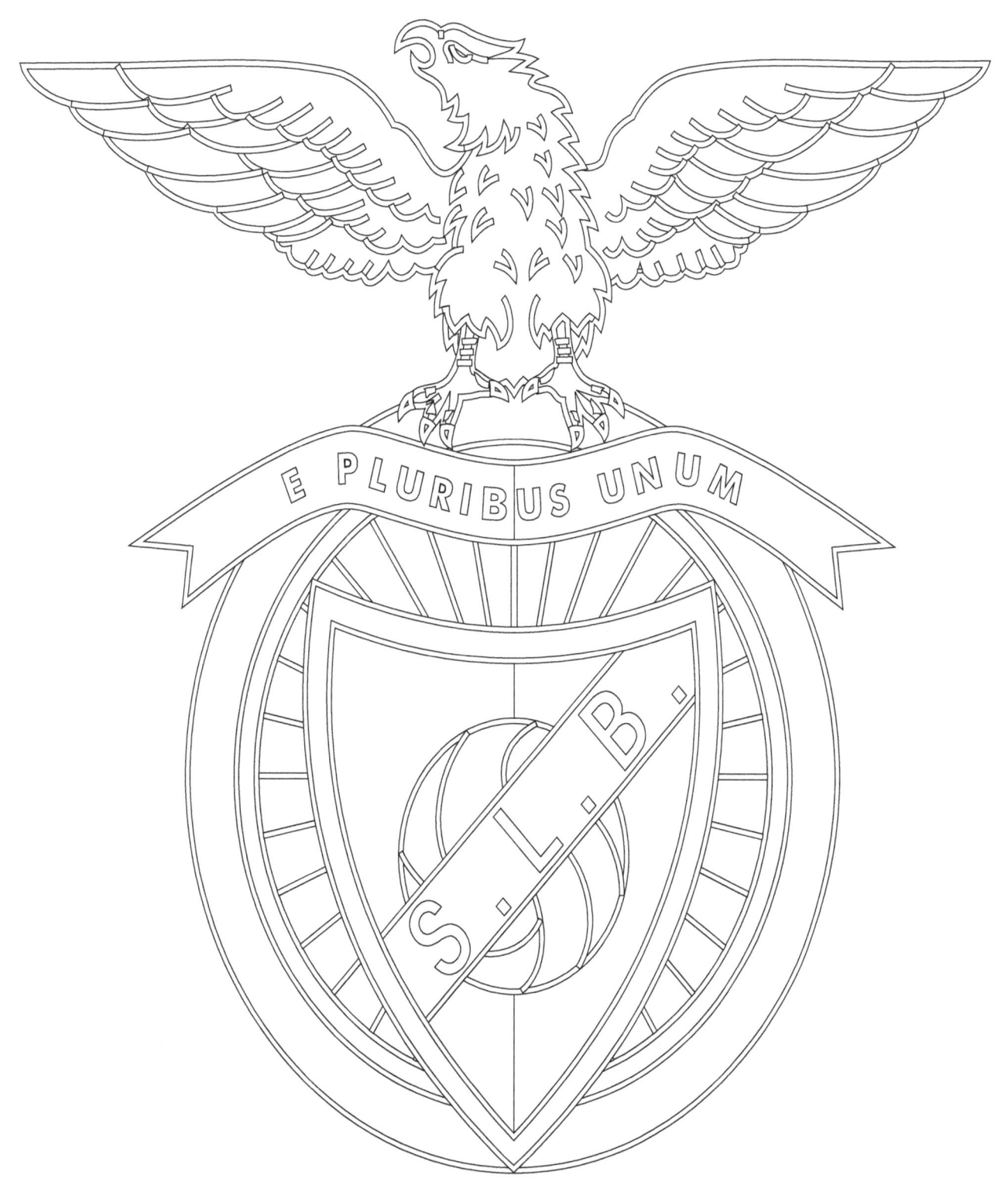

FC PORTO
Has Won the Copetition TwoTimes: (1987-2004).

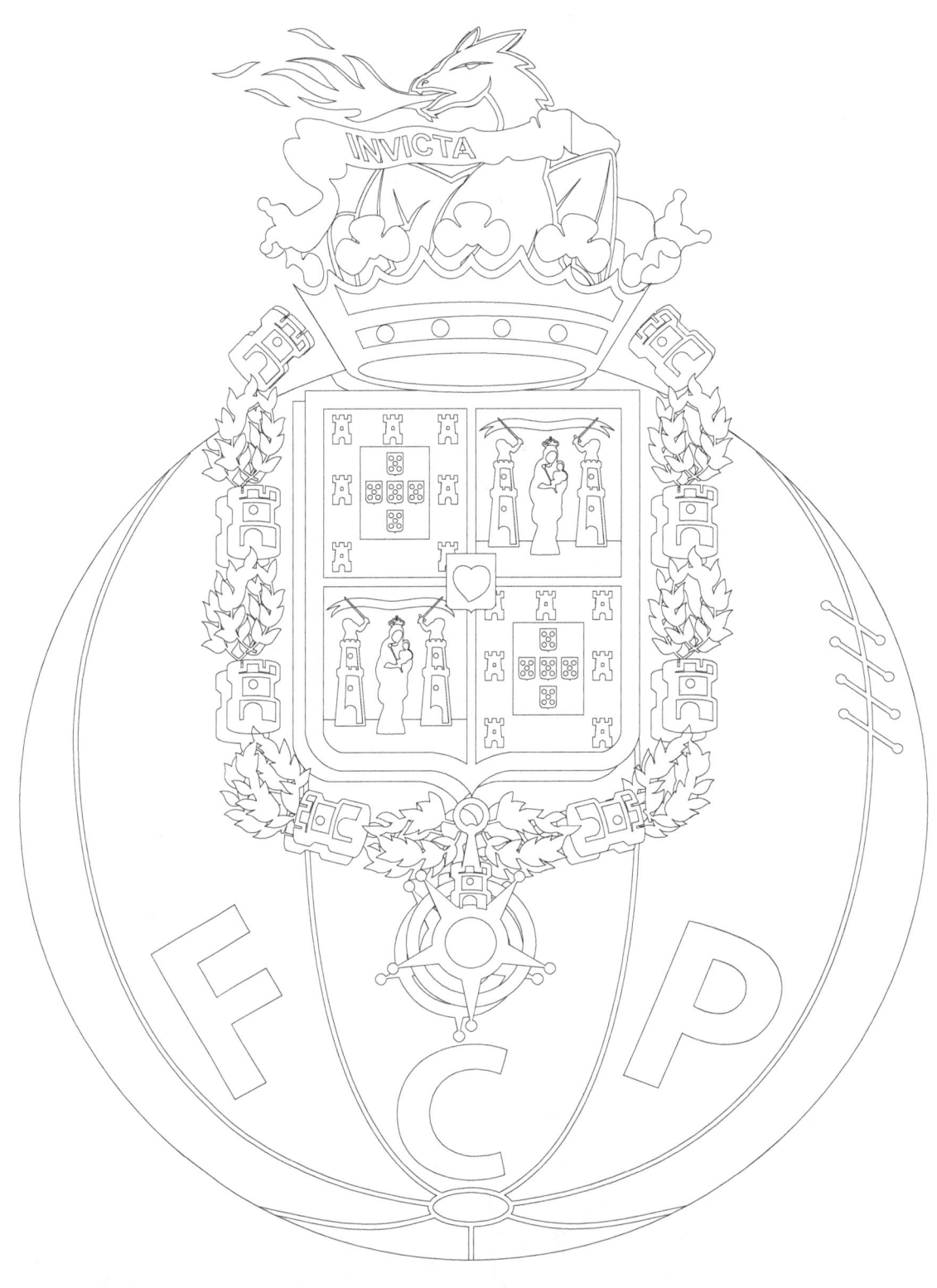

NOTTINGHAM FOREST
Has Won the Copetition TwoTimes: (1979-1980).

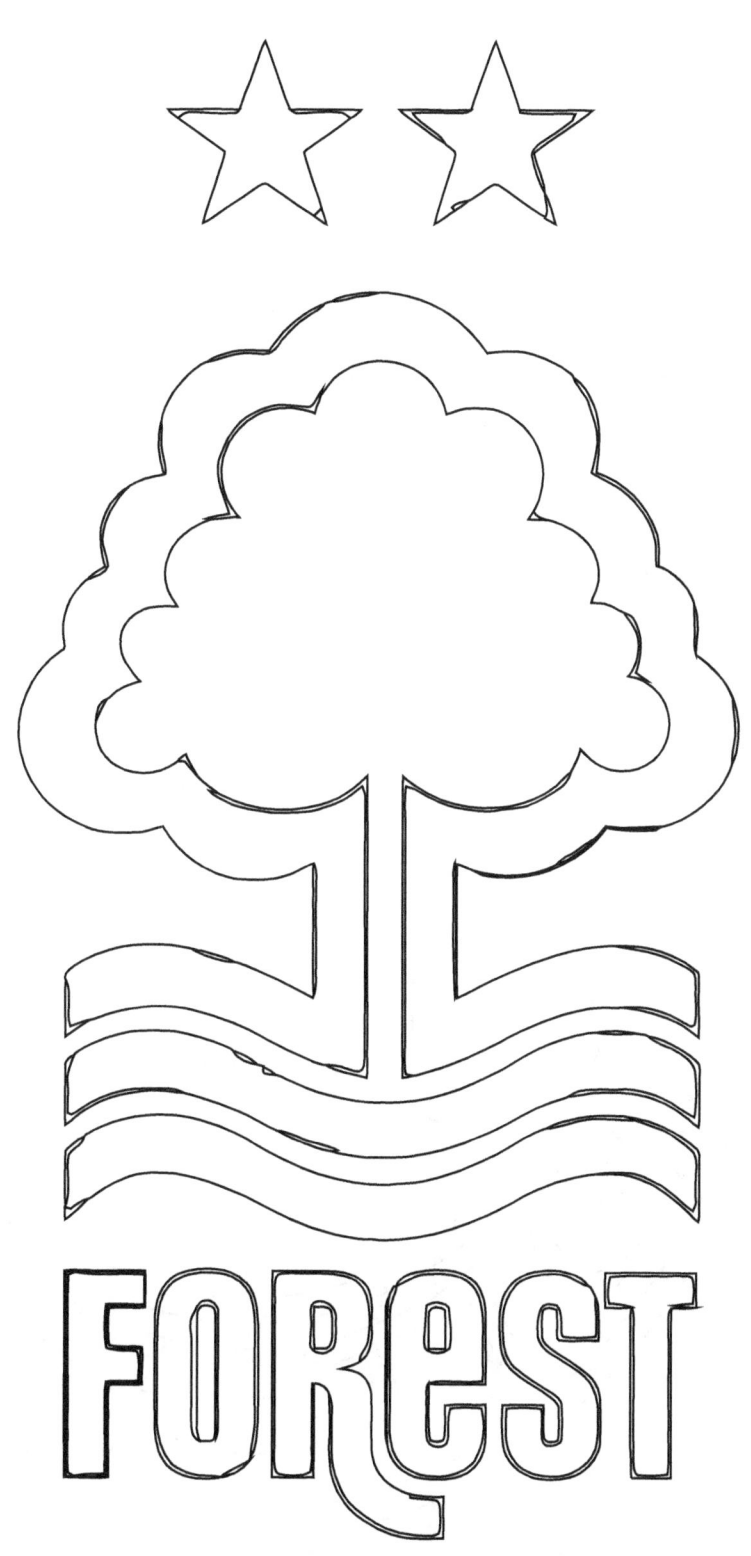

FEYENOORD ROTTERDAM
Has Won the Copetition OneTimes: (1970).

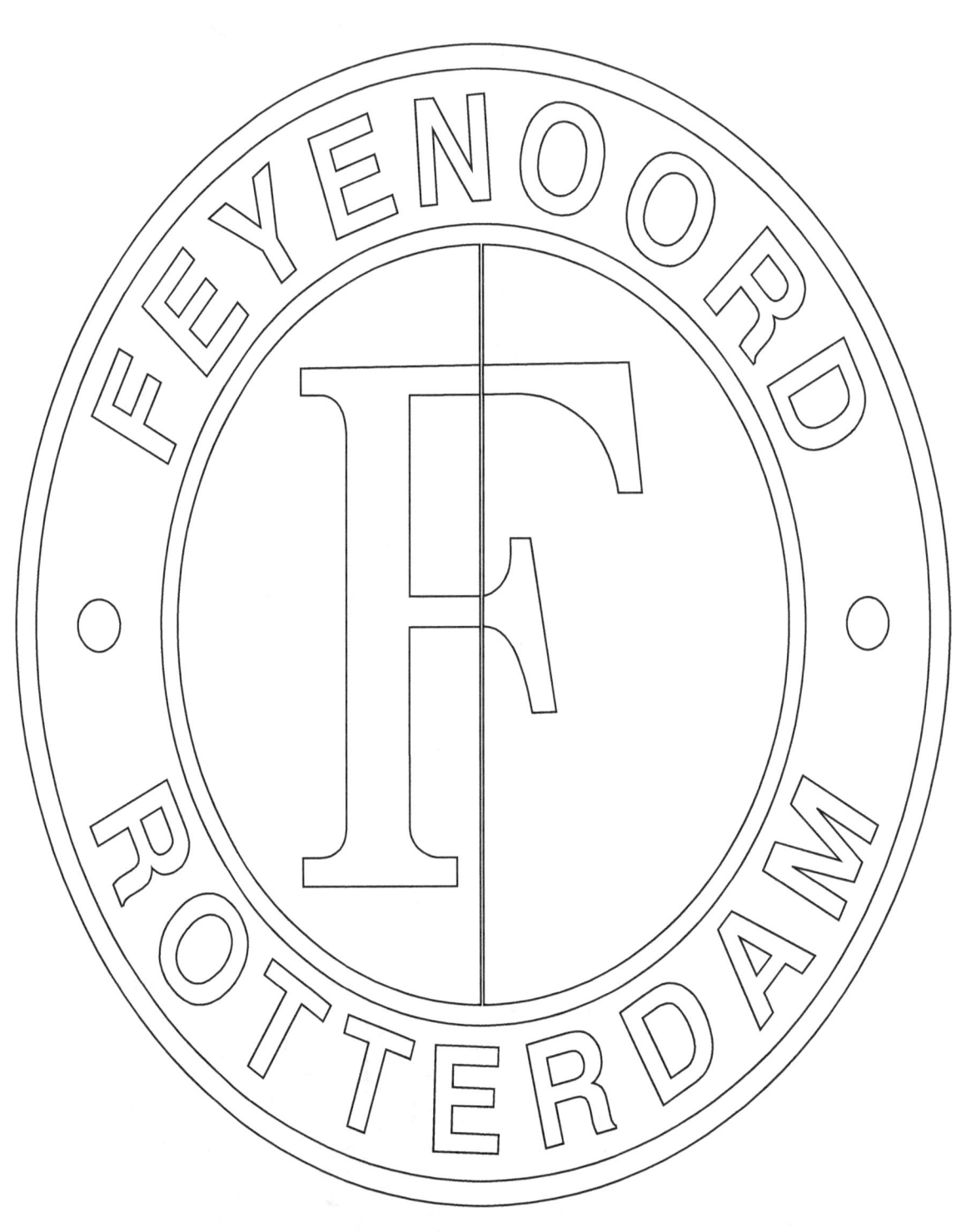

CELTIC FC
Has Won the Copetition OneTimes: (1967).

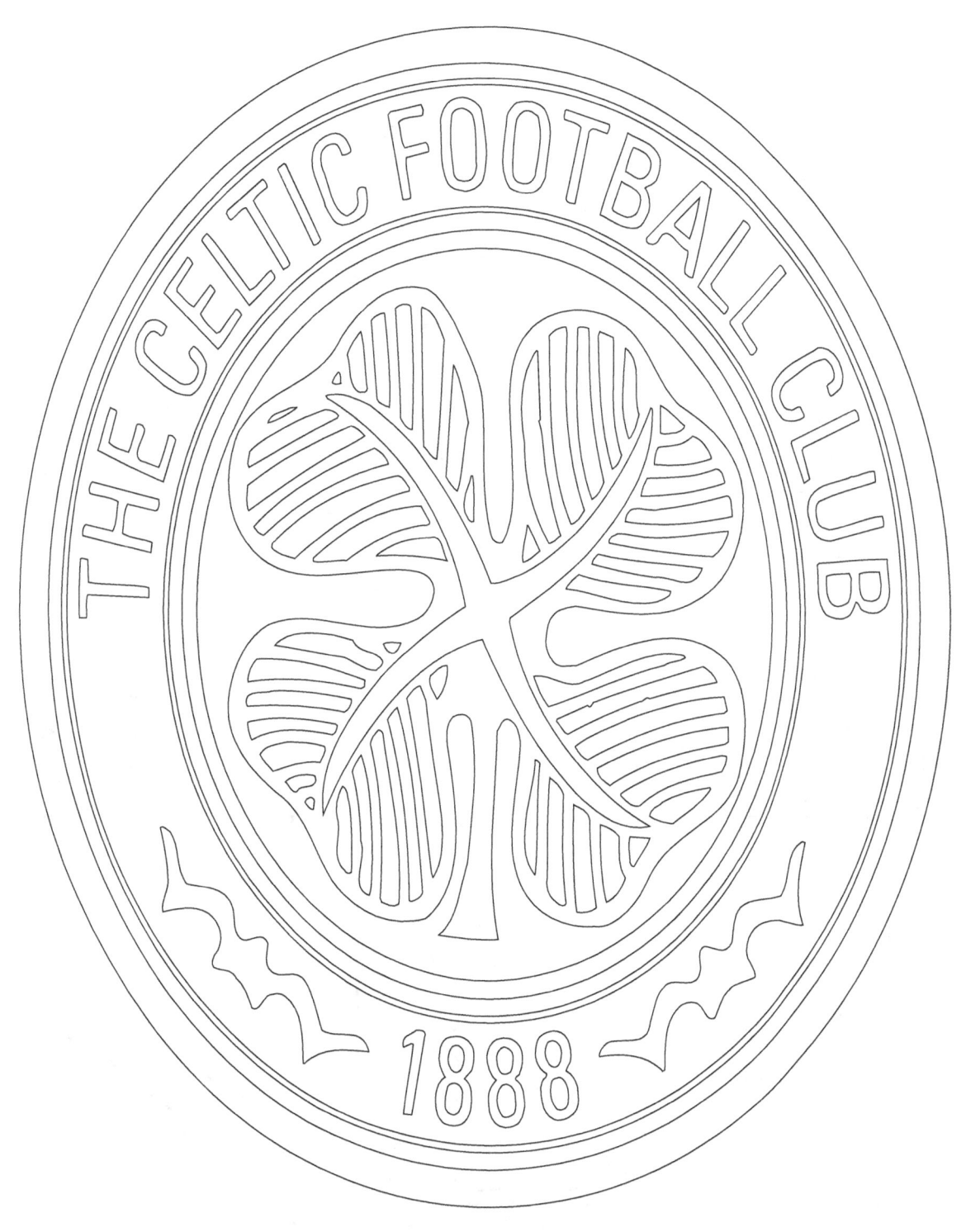

FCSB
Has Won the Copetition OneTimes: (1986).

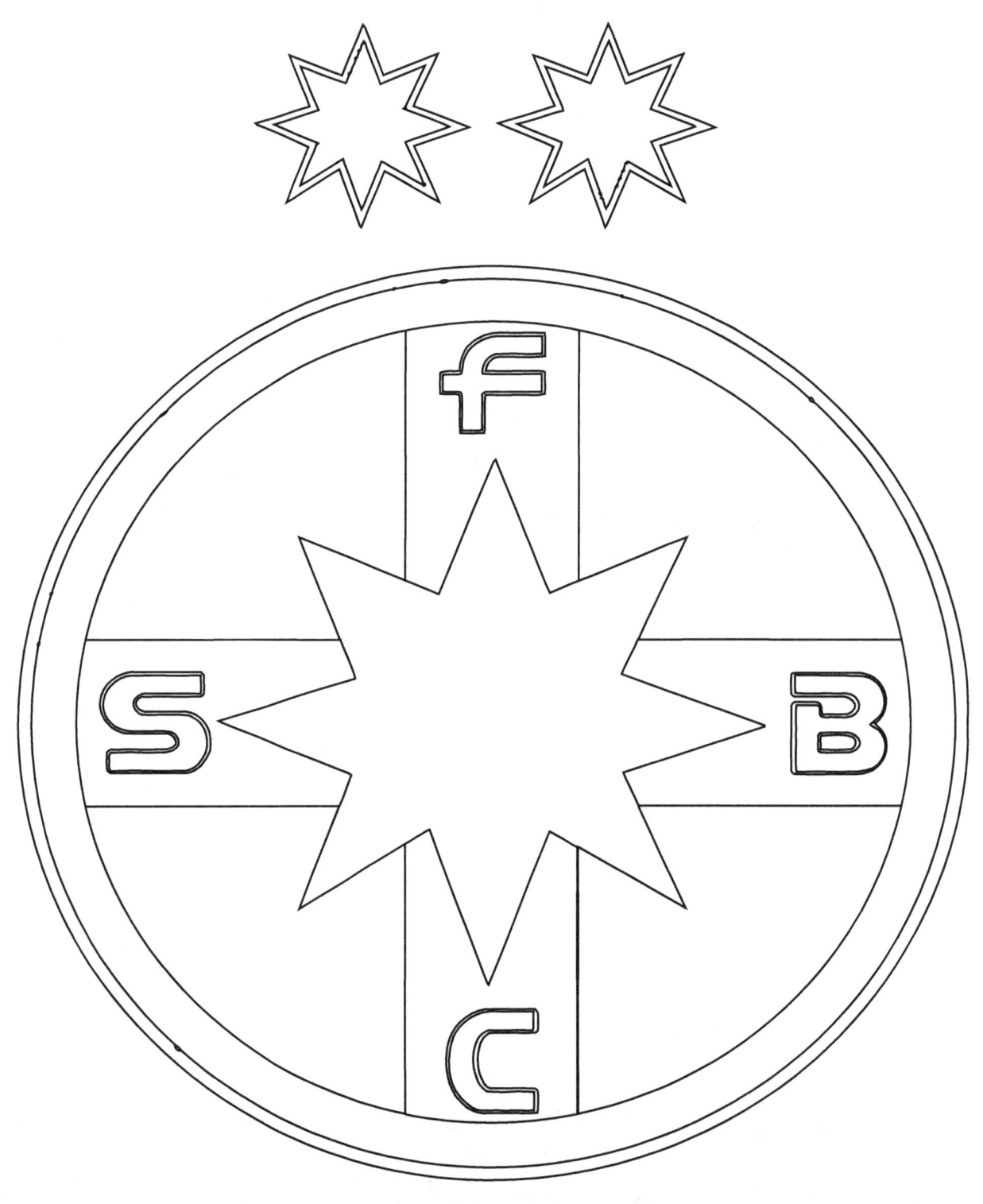

PSV
Has Won the Copetition OneTimes: (1988).

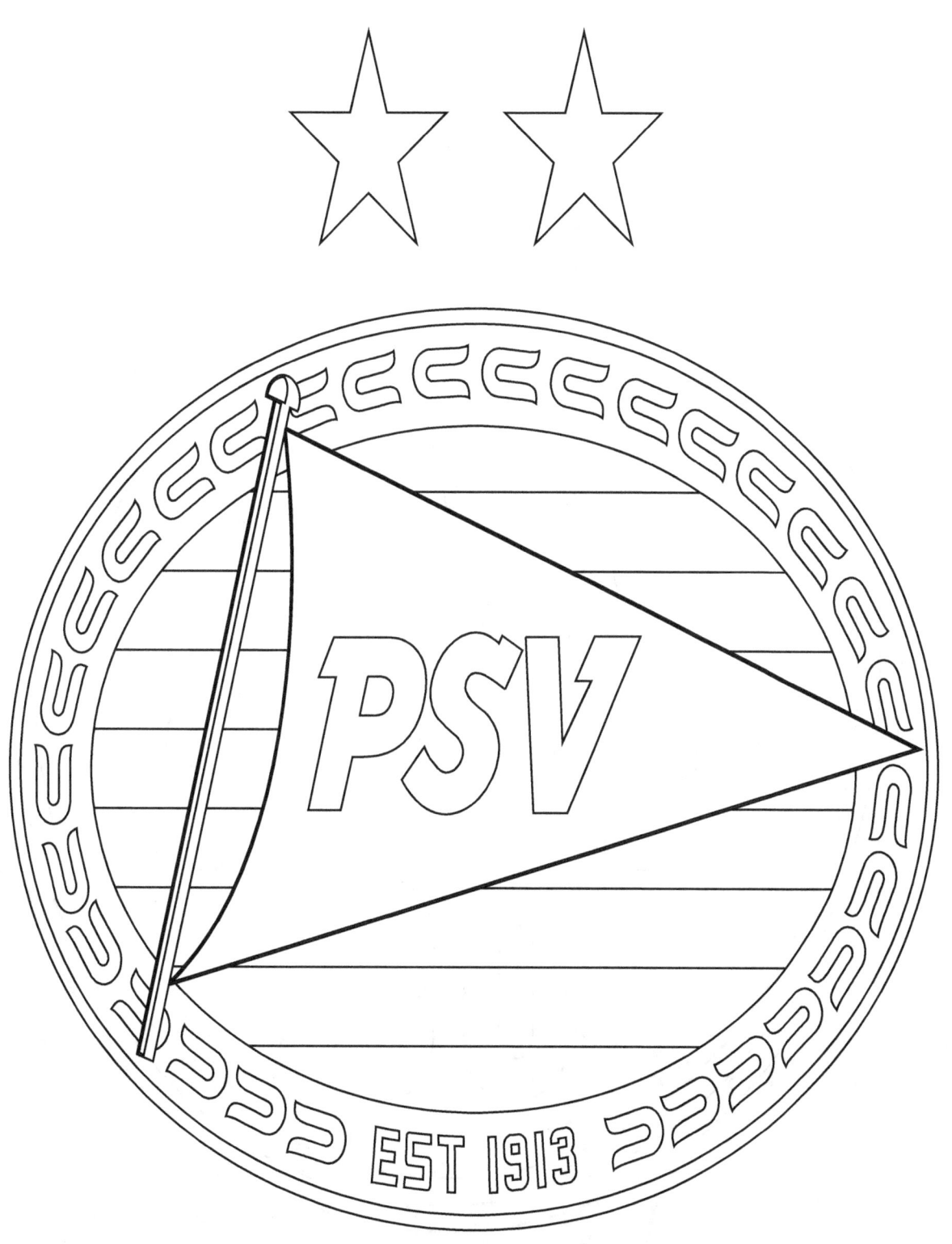

BORUSSIA DORTMUND
Has Won the Copetition OneTimes: (1997).

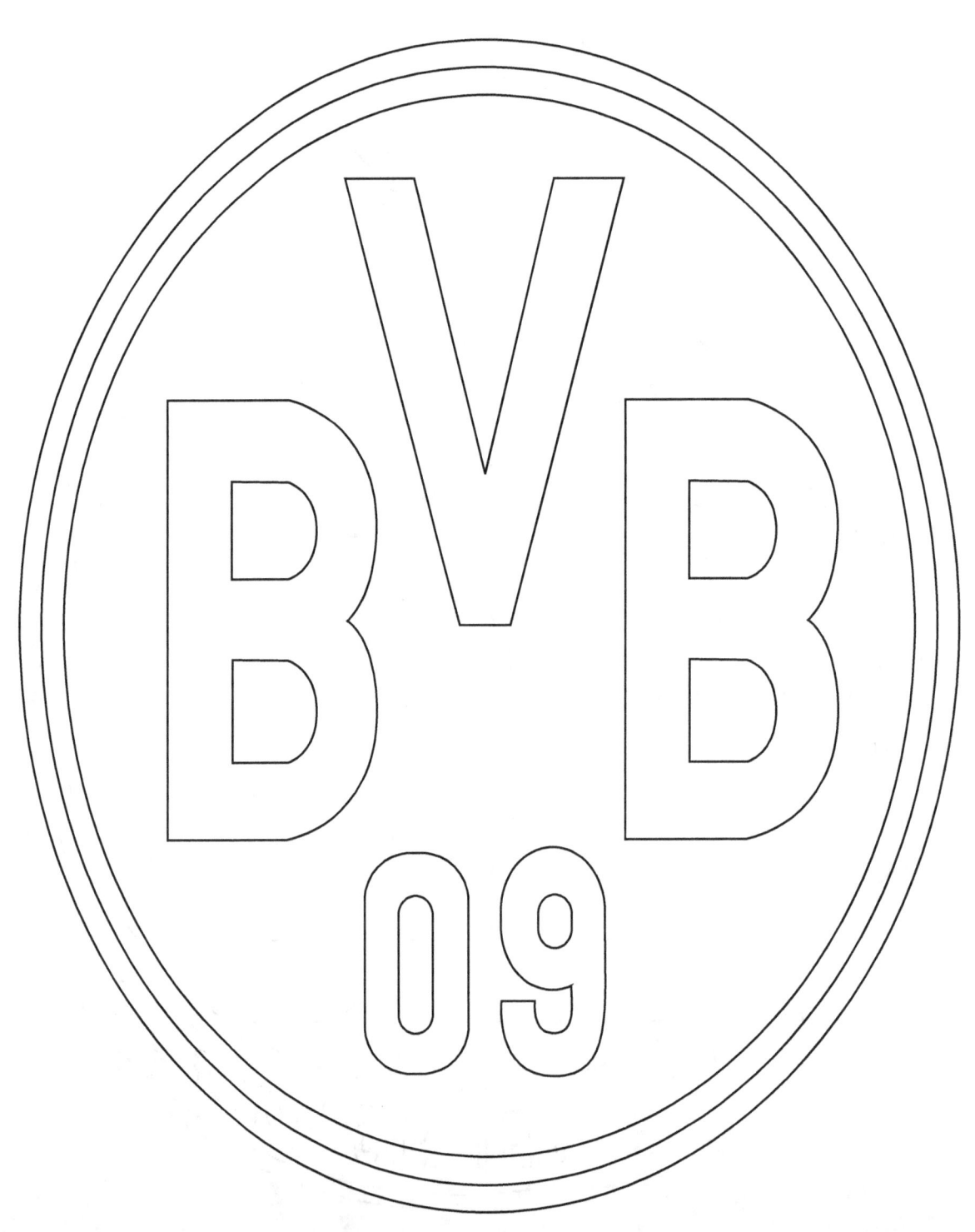

ASTON VILLA FC
Has Won the Copetition OneTimes: (1982).

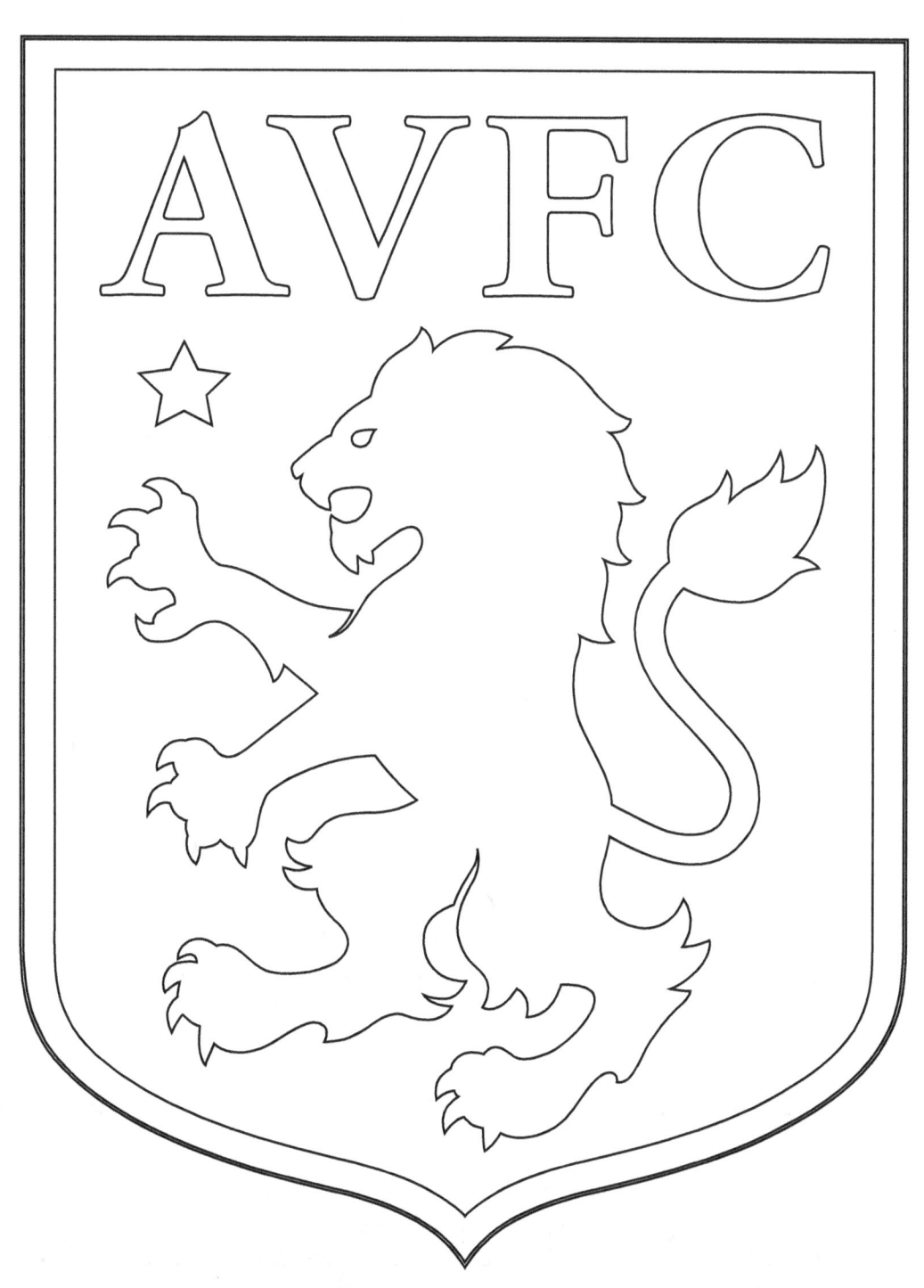

OLYMPIQUE de MARSEILLE
Has Won the Copetition OneTimes: (1993).

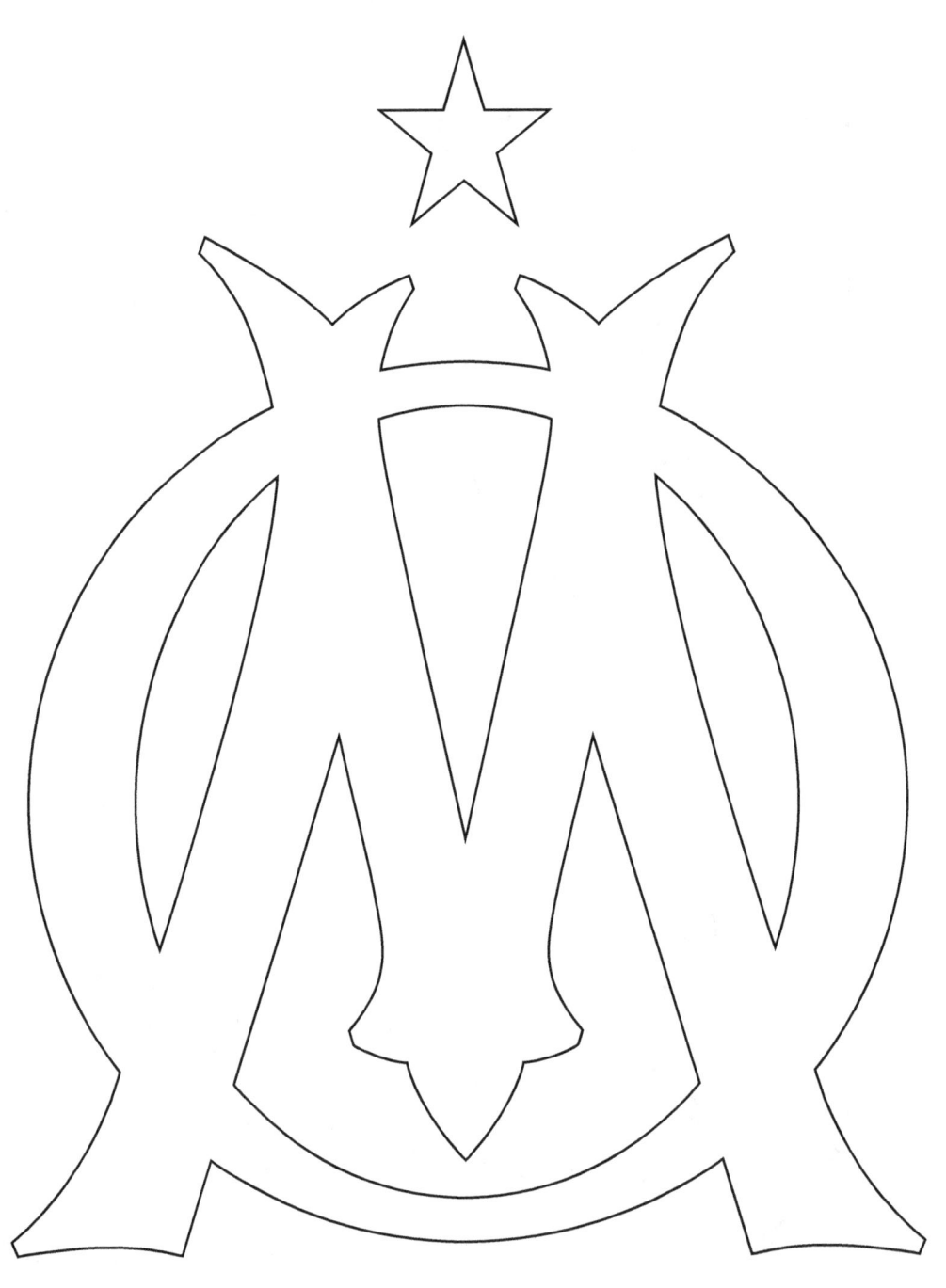

HAMBURGER SV
Has Won the Copetition OneTimes: (1983).

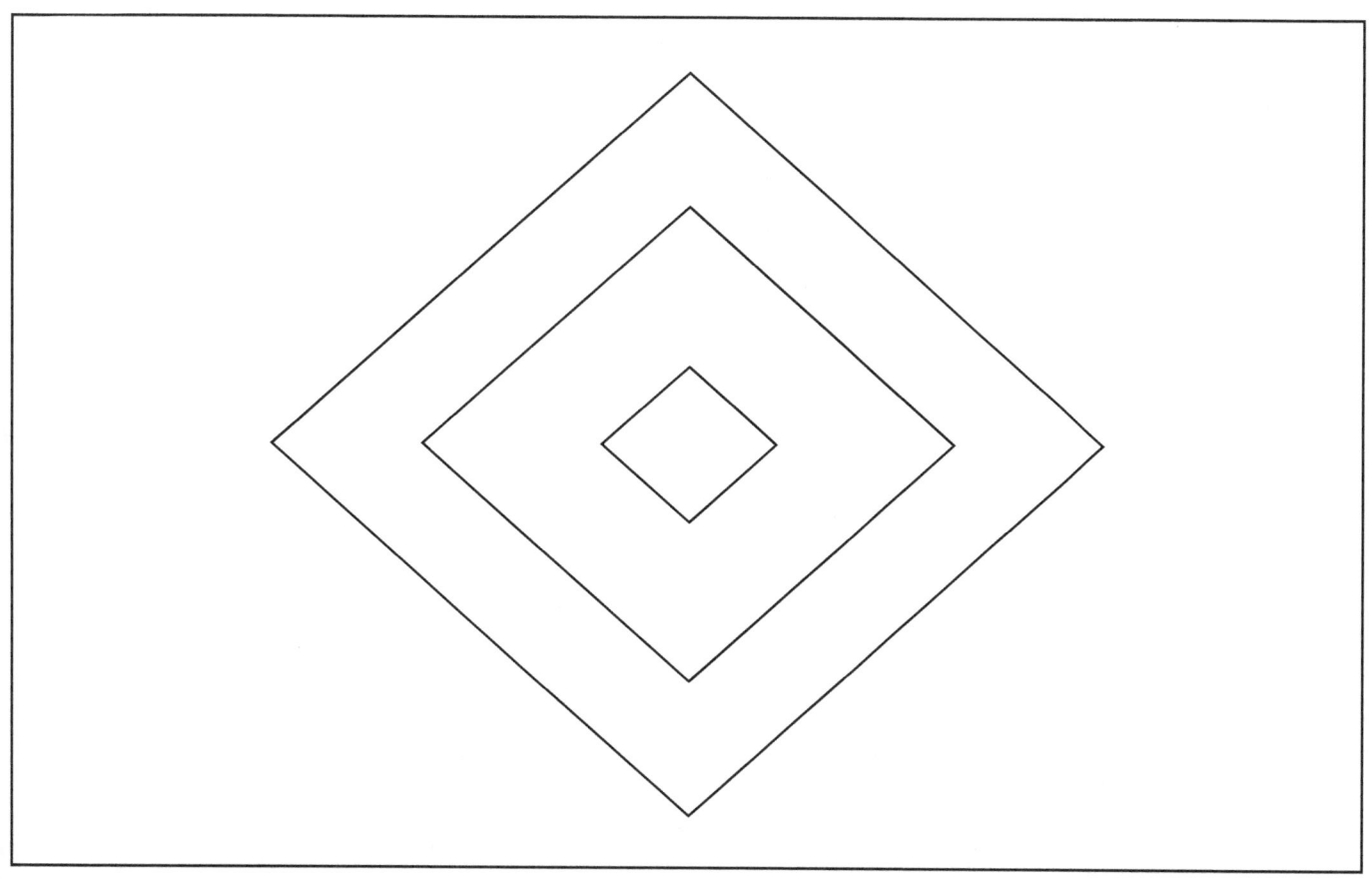

CHELSEA FC

Has Won the Copetition OneTimes: (2012).

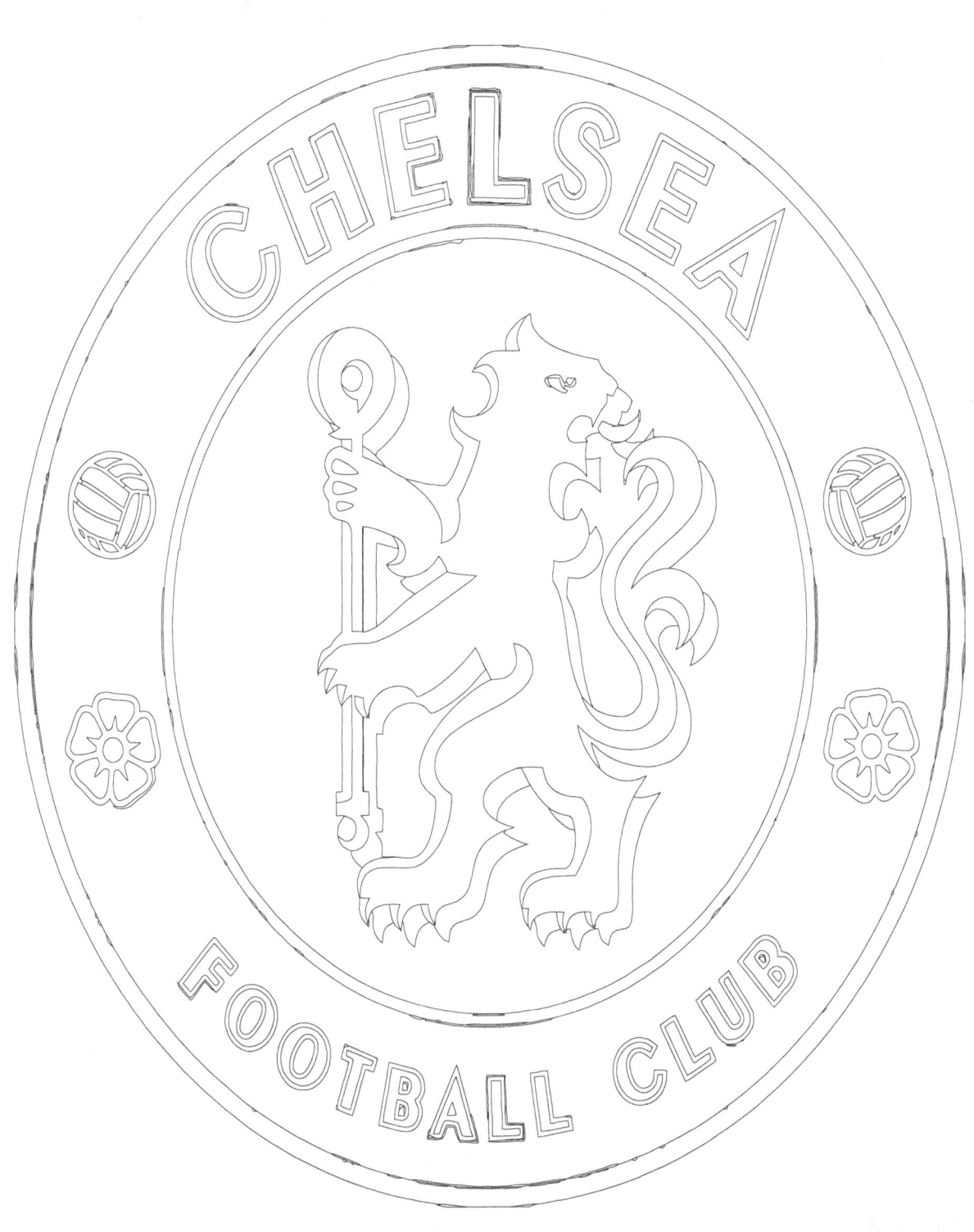

FK CRVENA ZVEZDA

Has Won the Copetition OneTimes: (1991).

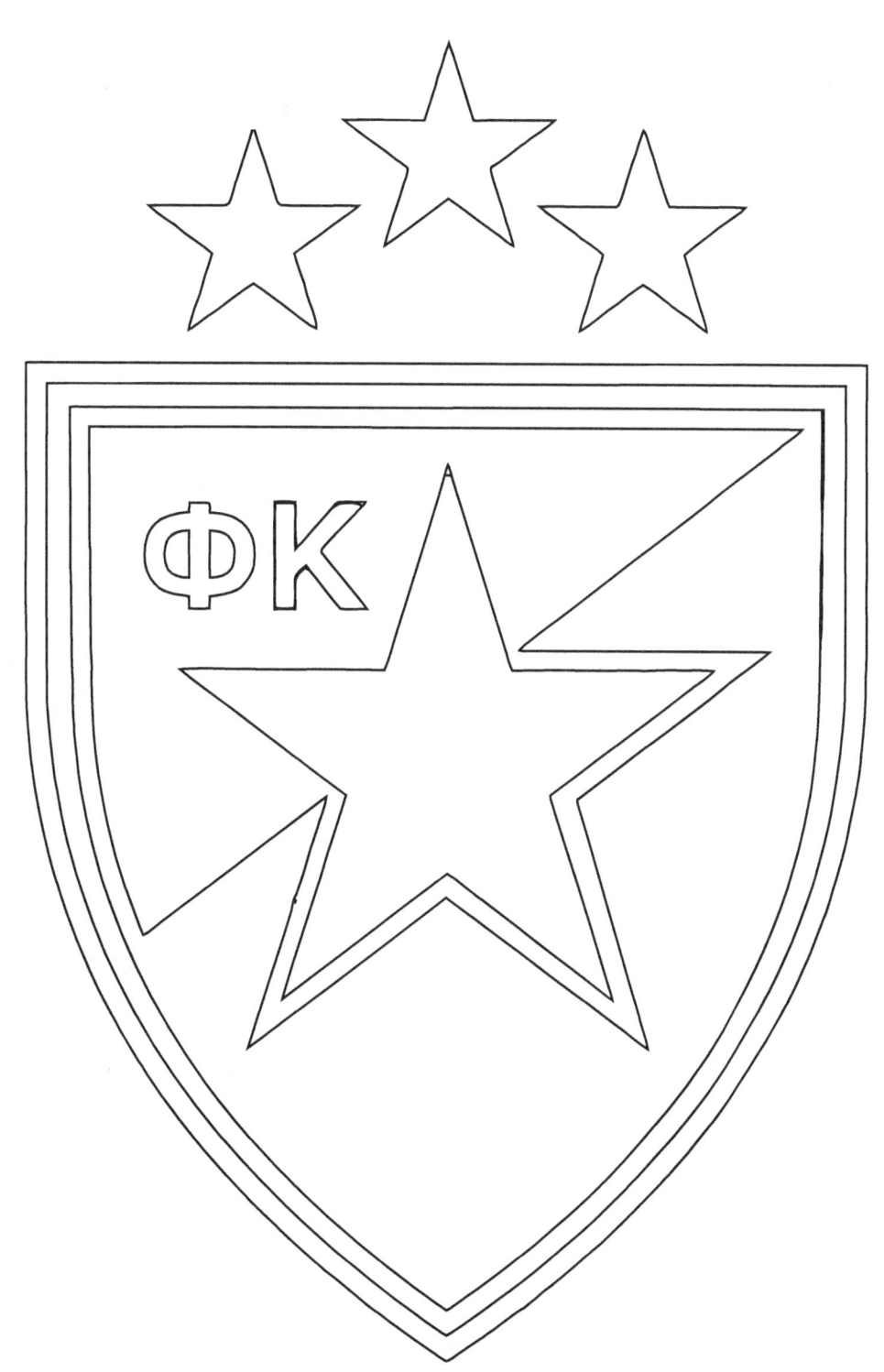

Guess Who is the Next Winner of UEFA Chmapions League 2021!

www.ingramcontent.com/pod-product-compliance
Lightning Source LLC
Chambersburg PA
CBHW080821220526
45466CB00011BB/3644